50 Simple Happy Tips

Noah Shelton

ISBN-13: 978-1537576619
ISBN-10: 1537576615

"Being happy never goes out of style."

–Lilly Pulitzer

CONTENTS

Preface

There was a time when life might have been a tale told by an idiot. Perhaps from the philosophical point of view that was okay. Although people in those days lived a life with an abundance of blessings, they were missing so many potentials; the term 'individualism' had not been too popular then. Time is a gypsy tribe. It never rests. The ever changeable nature of it has changed the lives of humans. Living has been remodeled with the passage of time. Now, life is not a tale; it is a diagram designed by the one who lives that life. Everyone is the engineer of their own life, but how many know this?

The term 'individualism' has dominated the life on earth too emphatically that everyone has become conscious of what is worth living in this earth. The meaning of living life is not only compressed within living a life, but it means living a life with some value in it. One can change his life with the magic touch of decision and determination.

Living in today's world is the most challenging living ever. The challenges of living have made life on earth complicated. People are trying hard to eradicate the complications, though with very little success. It seems we are ready to accept the complications; we cordially invite them in our life without too much hesitation.

A deliberate thought about a worthwhile life strategy denies the complication in life. There are many ways to say goodbye to the complications in life. We are the human being; we created the troubles. So can we remove them?

Happiness is subjective to the individual and their experience of that moment. With this awareness, you can choose to be happy consciously. Here are 50 tips that anyone can do at any time to purposely cultivate happiness into their life.

1. What are the processes to attain happiness?

Everyone craves a life full of happiness. What is the formula of living happily? Is this an abstract idea?

The idea of happiness can be best described by Einstein's Theory of Relativity. When most of the things around you are in perfect order, you feel good. A heavenly bliss is felt to see there is no trouble in life.

The best way to see things go on perfectly is to make things get done on our own. We must take responsibility for all the actions which somehow are related to us. To escape from the reality of taking burdens which would momentarily make one successful, by providing short happiness, in the long run one suffers when a bigger challenge appears. Stepping up to accept the challenges is not a heroic exploit. It is the duty of human being when the question is about existence.

We should stop pointing fingers to others for our own actions; we must be fit to take responsibility of what we did.

We must avoid anger. Anger makes us down in the process of attaining happiness. Frustration is the biggest enemy towards the path of success. Once we fail, we may not give up; success must be achieved and happiness must be attained.

2. Creation of new things and appreciation for what makes us feel happy.

Creation of anything new is always joyful. We are possessed with vast intelligence. We have the capability of creating something new. Whether it is a product or an idea that exists in this world, only we have created it. Life on earth has been improving with the practical use of these things. Just imagine you have created such a new one and brought benefit to the life of other people! Won't it be a wonderful idea?

What can we create? Do not bother to go for something very unique. Just concentrate on those which exist. Renovate them; use them for the betterment of life.

Let our creative venture be started from home. There are a lot of household products around us. Why don't we produce a tool in the kitchen which would help our mom to bake a cake with a little more ease? Add something to Grandma's wheel chair so that she can access it more swiftly. Ok. Are these ideas unfitting to you? You must be a facebook gig. Write a short story or design a nice picture focusing your friends be there, share it with them in a lay weekend. See their response.

We can create some joke, some ideas. These creations come to the service of others and this is the fun to enjoy. Now, it is the time to sit and decide what you will create.

The feeling of being a creator is heavenly. You may have created many thing as regulation work but you never have counted them. Count them. It makes us not only joyful but vigorous to try another new one, also.

3. Create your own idea; define things in your way adding some judgment.

We live with ideas. We define everything by whatever comes across our way to living. Most of the ideas and definitions are guided by the established views.

Those who are intelligent, make their own idea. They define things the way they look at them.

We live our own life. We are all fee wills. So, it is our right to put personal views on everything.

Not always our views or ideas and our personal definition would be celebrated by other people. A well judgmental view can even be refuted because it may contradict other's views.

Walk along the safest and the most accepted path. Make your own independent view accepting what established views are there. There are fewer risks to be criticized. You will be accepted by other people.

More acceptance will make you happier. It builds confidence. Confidence is the key.

Rejection of the established views makes one become a society outcast. People avoid corresponding with these kinds of extreme people. So, a blend of strong personal view and flexible reception of what prevail in the society makes a balanced personality.

4. Do not worry if other people become faultfinders of you.

We are always alone in this world. We came alone; we will leave alone. We form society to live a better life, to solve our problem. But, still, we are alone.

With the course of time, we allow people to come into our life. We care what they think about us. It is always the best idea to have some people around us who think about us and share their thinking with us.

Sometimes, this beneficial company turns to be an extreme critic of anything we do. This type of criticism produces us nothing. These people make us nervous. We get scared to put our next step. This fear of being criticized hinders us to move forward to success. This is the main obstacle in the way to attaining happiness.

Why do we allow these criticisms to influence our life? We are the lonely souls. We do not need those who cannot make constructive criticism. The sense of 'I' is present in us so, we can move along through life without them. Be careless what people around you tell about you. They have time to say a lot about you; you do not have time to listen to them. It is your prime time; take leap to the success.

Make a list of the people who trouble you too much; do not leave them; just avoid them. You cannot leave them because, perhaps some of them are socially too close to you; maybe they are your family members.

5. Be a child; be curious to know more.

Steve Jobs once advised students to be children in the graduation program of a university. Naturally, the brain cells of children are blank. In the passage of time, these cells are occupied with knowledge of new things. Steve Jobs suggested students to remain always hungry to acquire knowledge.

Learning new things is enjoyable. The feeling of a new knowledge makes us take attempt to do a new thing. Doing a new thing is always profitable from a psychological and economical point of view.

We should feel a sensation to learn. In our conscious life, we learn things to use them in our life. Much of our learning is target oriented. We gather knowledge to make ourselves fit for living in this world of competition. This practical purpose of learning brings frustration.

Target based learning sets a goal of achievement and when we fail to avail the achievement, we become frustrated; our happiness is disturbed by the thought of failure.

Involuntary learning is a kind of demand-free way of gaining knowledge. When we learn just to know or to purge our inner self, we will definitely be benefitted, and no sense of failure will appear. So, the goal of learning should always be to earn spiritual improvement, rather than some materialistic gain.

6. Make an effort to make people happy; watching happy people brings inner peace.

'Sacrifice your life for others.' Rather an extremist view, isn't it? We do not need to "sacrifice" our life. Just spending some time of our routine life for the betterment of other lives is sufficient. To see other people smile for our effort will make us have a broad smile for sure. That is a smile which always comes from our inside. Try this:

Be always in the first row when anybody asks for help. You do not need to bother for your capability. Your simple effort is the best help for others. Do not calculate the rate of profit-loss ratio before making the decision to help somebody. Do not even think about the consequences. Whatever the aftermath of your heartiest effort, never step back.

Just think about your own situation when you need help. You only get those beside you who received help from you earlier, who has a sense of gratefulness. Helping other people makes you confident of having somebody beside you when you are in need of them. This confidence will make you feel comfortable always; you will be relaxed and live a life more joyful than ever.

Happiness is contagious. This feeling can pass through soul to soul. It is a realistic process to become happy. Confused? You must be thinking, how does it work or, does it really work? It is not only realistic but also a proven process. Let us find our answer.

Why do you spend time in the garden among flowers? It is only because flowers, butterflies, and birds are the sources of color and joy. Spending time with them makes us joyful too.

Now take a look. Why do you think the Presidents spend time with school children? Do you think that the children will be motivated to be the future leaders? You are right, but only to some extent. The Presidents are fatigued from their heavy work load. They need to reduce their lethargy in order to be fresh. They come close to the children to be influenced by the natural joy that prevails in the kid's school.

You are a busy person. You cannot spend time in nature or sit among children because you cannot manage spare time for that. Remember, you are not alone at all. You are always surrounded by some faces either in home or at the work place. Some other people, like friends and relatives, stay close to you too. The list can be bigger. Stay happy with them, making them happy. Watching them be happy, you will feel immense joy in yourself.

7. Comparison brings unnecessary distress; never do it.

What is the real value of 'individualism'? Although we live a social life, we are always independent from our heart and soul. We possess what we should possess. The range and frequency of our possession may vary from person to person. It is not wise to compare our possession with what other people have.

Generally, life in earth follows a strict rule of balance. Without this balance, life on earth might have been destroyed by now. This natural balance has a control over our capability. Naturally, the more effort you put into any work, the more you will achieve. It is the basic rule of the balance. So, it will be unwise to look at other's success with disgust.

This comparison makes us crave what other people have. Craving is the primary reason for unhappiness. Craving makes us to despair of what we do not have. When this feeling becomes extreme, we lose our happiness.

Doctors say that the best way to keep away from this kind of mental disturbance is to count your assets. Like others, you must have had so many things. Start from now, jot them down to make a list of your possessions. You will be surprised to notice that you cannot stop listing too early. Good news for you, there are so many people around who want to have what you have.

8. Focus on what YOU can control and accept natural facts.

We cannot alter nature or natural facts. We can just live along them. It is wise to accept natural facts in our life.

We do not have control over natural events, like death. Everyone must embrace death. Let it come in its time, and in the meantime, do something remarkable.

Ageing and hair loss often make us distressful. These facts must be accepted, otherwise stress will not stop pursuing us. By the thoughts like ageing and hair loss, we become the unhappiest because we do not have a solution to stop them.

Why don't we avoid these stress when there are more rational views of life available? We should remain busier to gain more success, rather than thinking about ageing or hair loss. Many people spend too long time to research the ways to prevent them. It is simply a waste of time; it brings unhappiness to our life.

Do a measurement of how long you spend daily thinking or researching on these natural facts? Now, make another plan instead. Do you have a garden at home? Take care of the plants every day; install a new set of plant there.

Reading is a very highly recommended way to avoid useless thoughts. When you read, read with concentration. Try to write something. Whether it is creative text or your professional writing, you can easily engage yourself in something good to avoid something useless.

9. Happiness is a process more than a formula.

Are you looking for the ways to attain happiness? You must have had much research on it. By this time, you must have become tired of so many philosophical tips, or some meaningless formulas. Actually, there are no established formulas of becoming happy. Happiness can be attained after following or maintaining some processes.

Happiness is a process. One can only attain it though some practices. Take a look.

- Be always mindful. Mindfulness protects us from irrelevant thinking and doing. A person with mindfulness is always esteemed by others.
- Practice forgiveness. It is a very kind practice. Vengeance destroys happiness. Yes, we will always be intolerable against odds, riotous against tyrants, strict against the slipshod, but forgiveness is divine. Tolerance to human mistakes can develop more beneficial relationship.
- Be generous. It is a beautiful human quality. It is not softness or weakness; rather, it is the rejection to braggart attitude. It makes us more humane.
- Think positive; be positive. To be successful in life we must show positive tendency to every sphere of our life. Result will always be variable. The sun always shines, once cloud melts. Cloud is seasonal and the sun is permanent. We should be indifferent to our positive intent, whatever the result is.

There is no shortcut of attaining happiness. We should make it a process of life, maintaining the basic practices though they are not too easy to maintain. Your strong will is the needed qualification to see these practices done.

10. Bad things do happen but there is always a good side.

Our life is full of events of victory and defeat. These two extreme statuses co-exist in our life. One may not be successful at every sphere. However, no one is totally a failed person either.

It is wise to be hopeful for the better to come. An optimist always gets better output. An optimist is always positive. There is a brighter side in everything that exists in the world. It is our duty to find them for good. A positive thinker is not an opportunist; he is rather capable of finding good in everything.

As bad things can happen anytime, we should be ready to accept them. Mishaps are the regular course of action in our life. We must not be distressed for the consequences of what happened with us. If we use our conscientiousness, a silver lining is not to fade in the black clouds.

11. Keep fit following the basic health rules.

Happiness is a kind of internal reaction of all living organizations in this world. It works in our subconscious mind. Our brain analyzes all the actions happening around us, and categorizes them to find out the sources which make us happy. This action of collecting data and analysis of them depends on some factors. Our physical condition is the most dominating factor among them.

Ok, let's not make it too complicated. In simple, our body and mind work together to respond to the mental state like happiness and sadness.

Just consider making a trip to the exotic sea beaches of Thailand. You are well arranged to set out in a day. You are too happy and excited at the prospect of this trip. How will you feel, if you develop a 'sore eye', just at the day before your trip to start? You may have managed the trip with an itching sensation in your eyes, always wearing sunglasses. Won't it be a terrible feeling, an agony?

To avoid uncertain physical misbehavior, we should be careful. We should maintain some basic health rules. We should be more conscious about our health.

To remain healthy is the key to happiness. It is not something that you are chosen to be blessed with; rather, you will have to gain it through some practices.

12. Study health guides; be your own doctor.

The practice of following health rules is a kind of habit that we must develop. We must do that to stay fit.

It is not too difficult to practice a healthy lifestyle. There are some established ways to do that. We should be conscious about our health first.

Study health guides. There is an abundance of them in online libraries. We can start by knowing the diseases. We can learn the ways to prevent the causes of the diseases. Most of the diseases develop due to our lack of knowledge on how to prevent them. We should be more careful to protect ourselves from some easy-to-prevent diseases.

Health guides are not books. They are the tips. They are scattered around many sources. We need to collect them and study. There are so many online resources on health care tips.

We can easily avoid doctors if we know some basic heath rules to stay fit. It is always recommendable to visit doctors, but too much dependence on them regarding our health is not a good practice at all. We are the owner of our physic and mind; we should take steps to help our health by getting support on our own.

13. Teach young people the health rules; it will swing back!

There is no mystery about this. Having a healthy lifestyle is a practice which should be settled on from an early age. We should take responsibility to teach young people about the importance of keeping fit. Let the activity be started from home.

This is not an easy task at all. Young people are often reluctant to learn. When the facts are related to healthcare regulation, they surely won't get it. Use some techniques. Make it simple to demonstrate.

You know that young people learn too quickly and they learn for a lifetime. So, it is the best time to teach them some basic health rules. Do you know that you can also be benefitted by teaching your younger family members and young ones? But how?

Young people are very quick to make complaint. They are capable of showing odds in your behavior and attitude. On the other hand, we, the matured people, are very forgetful and offhand, especially when the question is about healthcare maintenance. So, whenever we show carelessness, they will show them to us; they will laugh at us. It is too embarrassing for us, isn't it?

How can we teach young people about healthcare? As this band of people is very sensitive and less responsive towards voluntary learning, the method of teaching them should match with their category. They should not be bothered with too much grave advice. They should be allowed much time to develop the good habits. Parents can play an exemplary role. With the passage of time, young people will get used to the basic healthcare rules.

14. Be Active.

These should not be missed. Now days, students are showing less interest in them. Activities are helpful.

Activities can be the best healthcare motivation to the students. It is fun because people of any age can join them too. Meeting many people of a different type is an interesting thing. The activities help us stay healthy, both physically and mentally. Activities are exciting too. Excitement in life makes us live longer.

We are, by birth, adventurous. Most of the activities organize some adventurous tasks. Mountain tracking and canyoning have too many exciting prospects. These kinds of activities help us test our limit. We become confident when we come to know our limit. It will be easier to take decision depending on our limit.

Activities like bungee jump and scuba diving would help us to defeat the fear. Fear limits our capability. Fear makes us confused.

The activities do not only benefit us physically, they also make us mentally stronger. We can learn so many things, like cooperation, punctuality, effective communication, and the most of all, we get very ready to take challenge. These mentioned qualities are always required to be successful in life, and success is the most dominating factor to attain happiness.

15. Stay calm; take control of your own sentiment.

Keeping fit means to remain fit, both physically and mentally. We cannot overlook the ways which keep us mentally healthy. Our physical fitness is not sufficient if we are mentally depressed or unwell.

The best way to remain mentally healthy is to pacify our mind. It seems, now a days, it is not an easy task. Life has become more complicated than ever. The complications of life do not allow us to live peacefully. There is nothing to be too hopeless about this. There are some proven ways to bring mental peace. Take a look at them.

1. Meditation. Just like your body needs and requires rest each day, so does your mind. Mindful meditation can reduce stress.
2. Be philosophical towards life. Your view towards life ultimately guides you throughout the whole life. Develop a better conscience, and get your conscience appreciated by other around you.
3. Avoid craving others' success. It destroys our spirit of doing things by ourselves. Do not get jealous of other successful people. Jealousy destroys our inner self. It makes us sick both mentally and physically. It also brings death.
4. Be satisfied. Accept that what you possess are sufficient for you. You may not have had more than that.

Mental happiness cannot be attained by medicine. It is a process to attain through some noble practices.

16. Increase inclination towards herbal.

We take medicine to cure our health related problems. Medicines have chemical properties. These chemicals affect our health. Herbals can be good alternatives for chemical medicines.

Herbals have very effective medicinal qualities. The culture of using herbs as medicine is very popular in China and many other Asian countries. Herbs are natural ingredients, and there is almost no risk of using them as medicine. They are easy to use too.

When there are ample natural resources to cure ourselves, why would we turn to the strong chemical medicines? Herbal medicines are even effective in the treatment of some critical diseases like cancer and cardiac problems.

How can we use herbs as medicine? Study some resources explaining the method of using herbs as lifesaving medicines. Although the method is a bit slower and the action is time consuming, it is effective. If you bother to study the method, take help from the herbal medication culture expert. The regular use of herbal medicines makes us stay scare free of the side effects of many popular traditional chemical based medicine.

17. Rigorously get rid of the bad habits.

Many bad habits do not allow us to live a healthy life. Bad habits, like smoking and drinking, have far too injurious effects in our life. We can categorize bad habits in two distinct extents. One of them is deliberate and the other one is unconscious.

We deliberately allow some bad habits in our life. We start developing habits like smoking and drinking, even knowing their bad effects in our life. When we become nervous or stressful, we use these to escape from reality. Soon, we become dependent on these, creating an addiction to them. It becomes too late when we realize or face the negative effects of taking them.

Working till midnight and waking up late is another bad habit which we develop purposely. It has so many far reaching bad impacts in our life.

The unconscious bad habits are not easy to be noticed by the one who develops them. Other people notice the unusual habit.

To criticize other people around us is not a bad practice at all. It makes us enable to find out our own follies comparing our actions with others'. But, it becomes a bad habit to criticize others when there is no judgmental view in that criticism. It causes nothing but animosity. It is a bad habit that we cannot often figure out how they dominate life! This habit makes us too unhappy.

How can we eliminate these habits from our life?

We know what the bad habits of our own are. Although it is not too easy to remove them from our life, it is not impossible too. They have been developed over time. They will take a long time to be removed. But first of all, we need to make our mind if we are ready to say them good bye.

Whatever the bad habits are, we can make a routine of them. This routine will help us to notice what we do to harm ourselves. Reduce the rate of practicing the habits. You will see that the rate is automatically decreasing over time. The routine will not have to follow by then.

Make your mind never allow bad habits to dominate your life. Once you take control over them, you would be capable of eliminating them from your life forever. Now feel how happy you have become!

18. Overlook the odds of your partner.

Our relationships are always precious to us. The voluntary relationship, like blood related relatives, will never demand a strategic relationship. Contrarily, the social relationship like, living with non-blood related person, is something which needs to be maintained strategically to move on with it peacefully.

Peaceful coexistence in a social relationship happens when we show liberal intent to our relationship. We must not find odds in our partner.

Human beings are not free from their flaws. We are not perfect. We are the combination of good and evil. Some may possess either less or more of one of them. It is rather natural to have flaws in any person. These cannot be the perimeter of maintaining relationships.

It takes a considerably long time to develop a social relationship. Other people in this relationship do not only relate to our social and practical life, but they also share emotion and feelings with us; a beneficial relationship is cherished which is totally divine.

This beneficial relationship can lose weight, or be broken if we keep finding the follies of our partners. Our partners depend on us; they believe us. If we hurt them, they get too depressed; they lose faith in such a holistic relationship. The depression ultimately leads this relationship to ruin miserably.

19. Make some special contribution towards the relationship.

When we lose faith in the relationship, we decide to discontinue that. We engage in another one in search of peace, without much finding the reason for our lost hope. Ultimately, we cannot become happy in our new relationship too. Why does this happen?

We are demanding too many hopes out of our relationship. When we do not get all of them, we become frustrated. Why aren't we making some contributions to our valuable relationship? Is it too difficult to make?

The best contribution towards the relationship is 'sacrifice'. To sacrifice is a noble practice. In the history of the human race, anything glorious was achieved through sacrifice only. What do we possess that we could sacrifice for the relationship?

In relationships, we can sacrifice our demand. This is not something which can be seen by your partner, but it can be strongly felt. We can sacrifice ego for a valuable relationship.

The sacrifices can make a relationship happier and better. Most often, it is seen that the sacrifices do not go in vain. The other people involved in the relationship consider the sacrifices to be appreciated, responding to the contribution of the relationship.

20. Schedule your relationship.

Relationship is a natural bond. It can be of any type. Naturally, a male makes a bond with a female to make a family and breed children. There are other kinds of relationships too. Whatever the pattern of a relationship is, it is important to carry on. There is a nice way to do that.

Stop taking relationship as a status. Take it as an organization. This will make your relationship grow.

What happens in an organization? A set of work is being done always to get some results out of them. Then some regular activities are followed to run on the organization. All the activities follow a regular schedule. A relationship can also be given the shape of an organization. Why will you do that?

In our life, there are lots of things to follow. We earn money to live well; we go shopping; we go to the cinema- all these we do for living. In our relationship, we should do these following a regular schedule.

Responsibilities can be properly distributed among the people in a relationship. Of course, do it after an elaborate discussion. It will prevent any debate or confusion to arise.

21. Make your presence in the relationship, rather than giving effort to prove it.

Let other people in the relationship feel your worth for them. How will you do that?

Develop a strong personality. Let it not precede others' ego by harming their interest. Our strong impersonal self can easily dominate other people around us for good. When we have control over our conscience, our personality will certainly bring us a successful relationship.

We should do something to make our presence felt by others. Making a contribution towards the relationship is the best thing that makes us stand distinct in relationships.

We should not force to prove our value in a relationship. One or few contributions cannot prove that we are something special to others around us. With the passage of time, our contributions to the relationship will prove our worthwhile presence. A happy relationship grows up on the basis of commitment and the value of staying together.

22. Be a good neighbor.

Once there was a happy time when our neighbors used to mean a lot to us. They had been our society and to some extent, family. We had been happy together.

Our life now prevents us to maintain relationships like neighborhood. The growing complexity of metropolitan life, global challenges, too much engagement in work, and etc. do not let us say 'hi' to our neighbors.

Neighborhood is such a pleasant relationship. We share our happiness and sorrow with them. Once, the first childhood friendship used to be grown among neighbors. How thoughtlessly we are ignoring this relationship!

We should be more caring towards our neighbors. Relationship with neighbors would help us avoid some unnecessary distresses. In our bad times, we should turn to them to share our stress to reduce it. We should grow that relationship with responsibility. We need them in our life.

23. Look for ways to help others.

We should always spare some time to make some contributions for the betterment of other lives around us. It is a necessary step towards attaining happiness. When we engage ourselves to bettering others' lives, we will remain free from the sense of guilt of being selfish. This sense will bring happiness.

In the method of coexistence, fellow feeling is a common property of our conscience. We should step forward with helpful intent when we see others in distress. We must take some steps to help them get out of distress. It is not only the way to make a beneficial relationship, but also a step towards attaining happiness in life.

Just try out how it feels to help people in distress. You can comfort them by giving your physical support. You can make them morally strong by standing beside them. Misfortune does not choose a particular person; it can appear in anybody's life. So, every person in suffering demands help from you.

If you think you are not capable of helping them as you are in distress too, perhaps, you are not right. You have a sense of supportive intent; use it. Look for the ways to help people; make it a habit. You are not doing it to get some mere compliment from people; you are a real compassionate person.

24. Create new favorable relationships.

Friends are the integral part of our life. They make very special contributions to our life. Their role in our life is undeniable. We share our happiness and sorrows with them.

We should make some beneficial relationships throughout our life. They effectively influence our living. We can be a friend of those who have adequate amicable qualities in them. There are many people around us. You do not need to make an attempt to make a new friend out of them. Let it happen and then, take steps to develop it over time.

There is nothing to hurry about to prove your value. Do something which is required to develop the relationship in a natural way. Make some contribution.

Friends give us confidence to our life. It is a much required aspect to live happily. Most often, we face some troubles which only friends can solve.

25. Help those who need help.

When you are in a distressful state of your mind, you should look around to find other people who need help. Does it sound awkward? It is an amazing way to find resolution to reduce our distress! How does it work? If we closely observe how other people suffer, we will see our agony is less severe than theirs; we will have many options to come forward to their aid.

Our living in society requires that fellow attempt. We need to come forward to the help of other people. Helping other people will make us feel confident. We will forget our own plight.

We can improve our social engagement with the real intent to help others. When we constantly turn around to solve others' problems, we will have faith in us. It will develop our confidence. Confidence makes us successful. We all know that success is the key to attaining happiness.

26. Believe in something bigger than yourself; make yourself happy.

It is believed worldwide that there is a power beyond the limit of human beings, a power which has enormous capacity to control the whole universe. This power is known as God somewhere and some people call it the mighty nature. Whatever the name you use, there is an existence of something beyond our limit.

We won't lose anything if we believe in God. We do not have to pay for this belief. It is not even necessary to follow a religion to believe in the existence of God. If you notice the doctrines of all the religions, it is seen that the idea of the existence of God is almost similar everywhere. How does this belief work for you?

Just look around. There are so many people who go to church to confess or pray. Some others go to their holy place according to their religious belief. It is miserable to see those who pay money to the spiritual mentor who claims to have a special link with God and can help you get your problem solved. Why do you think these people are rushing to these places?

They need help. They need someone beyond human capability to get their problem solved. They are in pursuit of God. You are not an exception. You also need someone to whom you can pray to for miracles and blessings. Ok, think of it in another way.

You are defying the existence of God because you are overpowered with the feat of human being. Just think about your childhood. Haven't you called God to cure your mother?

Haven't you wished for an awesome gift at Christmas in your sock? So, why would some silly earthly achievements change your mind?

Try believing God. And try happiness.

27. Believe in God; turn your economy fortunate by making strict rules and a timetable.

How can you make your belief in God profitable in your life? It's simple. You are attaining inner peace that makes you calm. Your mental stability enables you to concentrate at work and you will be more prosperous.

The belief in God makes a person able to achieve a rather disciplined life. You can accomplish some other tasks which are indirectly related to your economy. You will learn a better management system. A good manager can turn any economy to fortune.

A true believer of God makes strict rules and timetables following the discipline he may have learn by believing in God. The person who can make rules and timetables in his life will not be stopped from gaining success.

28. Do some spiritual practices.

There are two distinct sides of our living- materialistic and spiritual. Waaijman considers spirituality as an integral part of human living. He advocates it to be practiced by all to attain peace. What is the basis of this practice?

In social science spirituality is defined as the search for the heavenly designs. This idea leads us to the importance of practicing spirituality.

We are constantly in search of the ways to remove distress from our life. If we let heavenly ideas dominate our life, we will ultimately find the best way to get peaceful bliss.

Once spirituality and religion were one co-existing idea. But with the passage of time, especially after the world wars, the idea of being spiritual changed and mingled with the more humanitarian views towards life. You don't need to bother with the idea that you have to be religious minded to be spiritual.

Meditation is a good spiritual practice. It brings tranquility of mind. We can train or take control of our unconscious faculty of mind by meditation. Meditation traditionally means relaxation of body and mind, but in a wider sense it means to guide our mind to concentrate to a certain matter. We meditate to reach God too. It helps us to control our emotions like love and hatred. It is very important to control our emotion because uncontrolled emotion brings sorrow in life.

29. Set your goal.

As a human, you have vast prospect in you. You can do something great. You can set a footmark, making other people follow your path towards success. Set a goal. It can be a goal far away to reach. Do not become hopeless.

It is always advisable to set a SMART (specific, measurable, achievable, representative, and timely managed) goal which is practical enough. In a well-balanced and disciplined life, you will set the SMART goal. You will achieve marginal success by reaching that goal. It will be a regular practice. But, think for a while, won't this process of regularly attaining success become a habit, making it monotonous?

If you feel the same thing, set a goal far away to reach. Extend the limit of your capability. Read the success story of those who have made the impossible possible; you will get answer of that madness. Do not try anything unusually impossible or beyond human limit. Use your intellect to choose your challenge.

30. Take fresh air; learn controlled breathing.

Fresh air keeps our lungs strong. It increases our stamina. It regularizes blood circulation in our body parts. Fresh air is not abundant indoors. We must be exposed to the outdoors; a natural surrounding would do better. We can practice some controlled breathing.

Controlled breathing is a kind of complete breathing that makes us live stress free. We can use our abdomen to do a very controlled breathing. We can use upper abdomen and the lower part of abdomen to take breath. This process should be continued for 10 to 15 minutes at a regular basis.

What can controlled breathing do for us? Adequate supply of oxygen to our lungs makes us remain physically strong. It helps us stay away from some physical and mental distresses, like anxiety and pain.

31. You should do some work from tomorrow's list.

Every day do some advance work to reduce tomorrow's workload. You can do some work from your next day's schedule. That will help you to remain stress free of the work you will have to do in the next day.

It is very easy to maintain. Make a regular schedule of your weekly tasks. Distribute them to your workdays. When you do some advance works, you will get more spare time for valuable recreation, like visiting new places or spending time with dear ones.

When you see the works done earlier than your schedule, you will be happy. Accomplishments are always joyful.

We always need some spare time to make plans. It is only possible to save some time by doing some extra works in advance from our next day's list.

32. Read the story of the heroes.

Read the success stories of the people around us. The stories can be a great motivation in our life. We can find a mentor among them, making someone a model in our life.

Look around. You will see a lot of exploit of some people who have succeeded in life. There are some lessons which we can extract from their life, which we can use for our own.

From the global leaders to common man, there are always some people who stand distinct from others, making some distinctive contribution to the world. They can be the exemplary role models to our life.

33. Let your emotion flow.

Emotion is the result of bio-chemical reaction inside us. It happens in its time. It is a natural process. Emotion makes us worthy of being a great human being.

We should not suppress our emotion. Emotion leads us to do something awesome in life. Most of the creative works are the result of an emotional state of mind. We fall in love because passion propels us to do that. We become sad or frustrated because we are strongly influenced by sentiment.

We should let emotion flow like a river. It creates some memories in our life. We cannot forget the memories like falling in love or breakups. We nurture them because we are fond of memories. We like to live with them.

34. Transform your emotion to text or image and make profit.

Today's world is the biggest marketplace ever. You can sell anything here.

Turn your strong emotion to image or text. Look back at the process of how the artists and the writers do these. Learn the techniques and start making some.

Transform your emotion to power to win. Make this strong feeling as a medium of expression. Make it acceptable. People would appreciate your feelings, and you will get more confidence.

35. Constantly find ways to improve.

There is no limit of success. No doubt that you are a successful person but, find ways to improve your status as a more successful person. No one would show you the way, or existing ways may not work for you. Find the ways by yourself to improve your status.

We can start by renovating our personal skill. We may have had some good degrees. We are drawing a handsome salary out of it. Why don't we look for the ways to improve some professional skills? We can take a diploma degree. We can learn how to make software.

All the new attempts are prolific. Only you should take them deliberately. Do not attempt anything which you do not find interesting, even if they are very profitable.

You can make a list of so many qualifications which interest you initially. You can take expert advice from people who care about you. Now, eliminate the options which seem unfitting. In this process you will get something to start new. This process of improvement will make you stay free from the monotony of living, increasing your personal skill which is, at times, profitable too.

36. Every morning should start with a thankful note.

We have so many things in our life which we should be thankful for. We should look back to our past days; how wonderfully we lived them! If one analyzes one's life with positive intent, the event of success will dominate the analysis.

Every day, we wake up with a renewed hope of living another day. We should be thankful for those days. We should be thankful for the chance to enjoy another day, a day full of broad day light.

Look at the world around you. You must have some people whom you are bonded with. With so many of them, you have beneficial relationships. They care about your mere presence in their life. They count on your presence. Just think, once you leave this world, they will remember your presence, but someone will soon replace your place in their life. This is a natural order of the human race; their attitude to living. So, you have only one thing to do- be thankful for living another day.

Your living is blessed with the gifts of nature. There are air, water, fire, earth and so many other things which you cannot produce. You make use of them, reuse them, and recycle them for your own good. Life in earth would have been quite impossible without them. We have plenty of them around us. We must be thankful for having these natural gifts.

37. Gratitude is a confession.

We must be grateful for the things which we possess. We have so many of them in our life. We have wealth to live a good life; we have nice people around us; we are being loved by our Creator. We should show our gratitude.

Gratitude is a confession. Confession makes odds and evils weaker which stay within our inner self. Each time we become grateful, our inner self gets enriched with the same consequence of what confession does for us.

38. Gratefulness drives out the demon of EGO from inside.

We are the most generous kind of creation of God. We can practice 'Humanity' because we are human. One thing spoils our credit to being worthwhile of a human being: 'ego'. It is a demon that lives inside us. We cannot often control this demon because it is not a feeling or sense; it coexists with our conscience.

We can nurture our human qualities by controlling ego. Gratitude can drive out this negative faculty of our conscience. In a general sense, we can say that gratefulness is the opposite attitude of egotism.

Each time we convey our gratitude to other people, it makes us acknowledge their contribution in our life. Saying thanks to others makes us come closer to them. They will welcome us cordially to a beneficial relationship. They will feel the urge to do something more for us.

An egoist person, on the other hand, often becomes a society outcast. Among too many grateful people, he would look totally odd and would be noticed too easily. Ego creates division among people. It makes caste and race in the world.

A person who can control ego is a broad-minded person. A broad-minded person can achieve anything good in his world. They remain free from the ill feelings towards other people, which is key to develop a perfect human bond.

39. Make fasting a festival.

Fasting is the best way to remain healthy. When we do not take in food for a long period of time, our biological metabolism responds to certain effects which are benefitting to our health. The best benefit of fasting is weight loss, and the shocking benefit of fasting, found in research, is the increase in life expectancy! Insulin increases when one follows a regular schedule of fasting. The decrease of LDL cholesterol is another remarkable advantage of fasting.

In all the major religions, fasting is followed as a form of religious ritual. In a controlled experiment on the fasting people in UE, it was found that they do not reduce weight after a month long fasting, but their cholesterol level was controlled with amazing results! The 'acceptable fast' is observed in many churches with a result that the clergymen are always healthier than the other who considers it as an extreme religious observance.

We are developing some diabetes problems and cholesterol risks only by accepting so many calories in our diet list. Foods are the source of many other diseases. We cannot avoid food; we can minimize the rate of eating.

Fasting is a controlled way to curtail calories from our diet list. It is not easy to achieve a practice like fasting. We should be determined to make it a festival of our life.

40. Create a morning routine.

Success in life depends on the good use of morning time. Look around to see how the successful people pay special attention to plan their morning.

A morning can be started with the following rituals. This way of starting a day is always motivating.

If your morning starts with the practices of some good habits, there is a possibility that the whole day will go well. You can focus on your daily activities early in the day before anything else perturbs your attention.

Wake up early in the morning. It will make you have a bigger day to work out your tasks. Drink a lot of pure water. It is a healthy practice.

Do some mental and physical exercise. Meditation or spending some lonely moments can be very good as mental exercise. Physical exercise keeps us healthy and fit. Do not ignore them.

41. Live a balanced life in all areas.

Manage your time. It is necessary to keep balance in all the actions of our everyday life. Thomas Merton considers a balanced life to be rather a happy life. We can attain happiness by making a good balance between our physical, perceptual, mystical and social life.

We must avoid too much rest as it develops laziness. Active and fit people remain happier than those who spend time in laziness. To have a fit and healthy physique, you should do some exercise. Avoid bad habits like taking too much alcohol and smoking. Get adequate rest. Sleep sufficiently. Find some time to relax and ease the pressure of work. Eat healthy food. Learn about some basic dietary facts. Spend some times with your hobbies regularly. Practice them.

Read various sources to develop your knowledge. Books are the best source which allow you to gather knowledge. At times it is not interesting to read books, but over time, you will be able to develop a liking for reading. Try to write something as well. It will be very good if you start with a diary entry, keeping the bulletin of your day to day activities. Soon, you will discover that you have so many things to write about.

By praying we can keep our inner self clean of moral impurities. We can read the holy books of various religions. Meditation keeps us focused.

42. Do not be over anxious about diet.

The fact related to being overweight has been the mostly talked about feature in 21st century as people are gaining more and more weight. It is said that the weight on earth has become doubled in last 100 years. People are being suffered physically, due to this increasing overweight problem. Diseases connected to cardiac and irregular blood pressure are the consequence of being overweight.

There is nothing to be too overpowered about this problem. Overweight is a kind of problem which we develop by ourselves. We do not keep an eye on our diet list early on, and become hyper when we gain a weight which we cannot carry. We become frustrated by seeing so many worrying results around us, and welcome stress in our life. Most often, we become too fretful about our diet.

We can easily avoid this problem by raising our consciousness early on. We can set a list of balanced diets and follow this. There are nutrition experts to help us in this matter.

43. Do not overindulge in one thing.

It is a kind of attitude towards life that makes us concentrate in one problem only, perhaps with little resolution, thus making us distracted from our valuable activities.

Some people show extremist view towards life by overindulging to one thing only. It is good to concentrate at one thing at a time. But, dissipation of our concentration is not good at all. It makes us ignorant of the world and the facts around us.

44. Study measures for a healthy lifestyle.

Do three things on a regular basis- eat, sleep, and exercise. You can call them three-fold paths of living a healthy life.

We can improve the physical factors of living, following some practicable rules. They increase our life expectancy along with better living.

It is not too difficult to achieve a healthy lifestyle. It is only a matter of our determination whether we want to live well.

Successful people have always dignified their life with the ways to live healthy. A healthy lifestyle is a result of a balance in life. This balance must be made on our own.

45. Take a walk.

The best exercise most people can do any time is to walk. Walking to our destination helps to reduce weight. You will get much more time to contemplate your life during a lonely walk to you destination.

Avoid lift. It is a laborious job to take stairs, but this is a good habit to reduce extra weight even without doing some traditional exercise. It will make you be physically active.

46. There should not be any compromise with sleep.

A sound sleep makes us rejuvenated. For all people, sleeping well is a thing you must maintain. You cannot avoid sound and timely sleep, even if you do not have much time to do that.

Modern lifestyle makes us negotiate with sleeping time. This is not a judgmental step towards achieving a healthy lifestyle. This practice makes us fall in illness both physically and mentally.

An adult must have a period of 7 to 8 hours of sleep every day. The best time to have a sound sleep is at nighttime. It is the time when we are not disturbed during sleep. A sound sleep is determined by quiet and undisturbed environment. Night is the traditional timing for the sleep of most of the creatures, except some of the nocturnal ones.

Sleep helps us to regain our physical and mental energy which we lose during our day work. Sleeplessness creates a state of lethargy, both in body and mind. This can cause stress. A regular and timely sleep can reduce this.

47. Make a constant habit of sound sleep from early life.

Sleeplessness traditionally refers to insomnia. Insomnia is a state related to sleep, which is developed for witless overlooking sleep, or not maintaining time. This often becomes a disease which causes strain in our life.

We can avoid this illogical trouble by making a regular schedule of sleep. Most of the people ignore the importance of sleep for not knowing the consequence of it. Other do it deliberately. We should make our mind first. We should not trouble our sleeping time with the daily works. We may not take an extra burden of work.

It would be foolish to occupy the schedule of sleeping with other tasks. We would have much more time to complete them if we sleep well and get ready to face a new day. If we finish our works timely, we may not have to work late till midnight, disturbing our sleep.

Our brain starts malfunctioning from the lack of sleep. Sleep is a metabolic stage when our brain takes rest and sets functional data orderly. If this function is disturbed by sleeplessness or untimely sleeping, the restoration process will be disturbed and valuable data will be lost. This is how the brain becomes duller.

We should practice early to bed and early wakeup from the early stage of life. Elders should play vital roles to help younger people develop this habit. Young people should be motivated to develop this action. Late night parties should be avoided. Drinking alcohol and overeating at night should also be made prohibited in life.

48. Make a habit of reading a book; it will make you have sound sleep.

Many people cannot cope with the busy schedule to spare sufficient time to sleep. As a result, they try to compensate their sleep at daytime. This is the reason they develop insomnia. Some other people cannot sleep timely because of the disturbing thoughts, or they get too stressful. Reading a book can help them to have sound sleep.

Take a book of any type. Start reading it. Do not bother whether it is interesting. You will see a miracle effect of it; you will fall asleep!

How does it work? Insomnia does not allow you to make a link between your body and mind to fall asleep. Reading a lighter book or magazine can do that.

Taking a shower or meditating before sleep can also help.

49. Celebrate the national and international days; celebrate special events.

The sense of nationalism can make us better citizens of a nation. It is important to learn the value of living in the certain location. A kind of responsibility grows among us for this sense which makes us do something for the respective nation and the people of the nation.

Celebration of the national days makes us know about the facts of our country. It makes us aware of the culture, history and constitution of our country. Knowledge on these three things will lead us to live a conscious life, a life worthy of living with responsibility towards the country.

We should observe international days and special events around the world. This will enable us to be conscious of the international facts. This will make us learn a lot of things from the days and the events.

By following the days and the events, we can know about the different cultures and lifestyles of people around the world without visiting other countries.

This can help us in another way too. By following the days and the events, we can remain busy in this good practice, diverting our mind from the stressful works.

50. Believe. Have the courage.

Self-belief is the key to success. It will help you to see the fortunate sides of living. It will never allow you to become discouraged. You will find more resolution of most of your problems.

Believe in the power of your own. You are a strong human being worthy of achieving anything. It will stimulate your power of doing new things in life.

Never lose hope. Have the courage that this world is simply designed for human mechanism. You are an engineer here. Why would you spoil your chance?

Set a goal to be successful. Make a rather bold one. Use your judgment to make it achievable. Develop your skill to be competent. Do not waste time thinking about the complications of life. You have all the possible ways to control them with your power of being a human being.

From Noah...

Living a happy life is a matter of choice. It's not what happens to you, it's how you feel about those events. In life, pain is inevitable but suffering is optional. Bad things will happen, but so will good things. Focus on the good things and cast away your judgments, faults, and problems to celebrate happiness.

Come back to these 50 Happiness Tips time and time again. It was a real joy creating this book. I hope that you found some of the tips helpful and can find ways to implement them into your life. I'd love to hear about your experiences and how things are going!

I wish you the very best,
Noah